The Impact on

Algebra vs. Geometry

of a Learner's Ability to Develop Reasoning Skills

by

Dr. Lisa A. Johnson Q .M.E

The Impact on
Algebra vs. Geometry
of a Learner's Ability to Develop Reasoning Skills

Copyright © 2021 by Dr. Lisa A. Johnson Q.M.E
All rights reserved. No part of this book may be reproduced or transmitted in any form or by any means, electronic or mechanical, including photocopying, recording, or by any information storage and retrieval system, without written permission of the publisher.

MAPLE LEAF PUBLISHING INC.
3rd Floor 4915 54 St Red Deer,
Alberta T4N 2G7 Canada
General Inquiries & Customer Service
Phone: 1-(403)-356-0255
Toll Free: 1-(888)-498-9380
Email: info@mapleleafpublishinginc.com

Because of the dynamic nature of the Internet, any web addresses or links contained in this book may have changed since publication and may no longer be valid. The views expressed in the work are solely those of the author and do not necessarily reflect the views of the publisher, and the publisher hereby disclaims any responsibility for them.

ISBN
Paperback: 978-1-77419-083-8
Ebook: 978-1-77419-084-5

This book is dedicated to my nephew,

Richard Dale Johnson-Dorsey

Abstract

This paper examines the impact that the reasoning skills: number sense, structure sense, and abstract reasoning, may have on algebra and geometry. The review of the literature is the result of perusal of more than twenty research papers, followed by construction of the accompanying annotated bibliography. The study was original research comprised of quantitative data collected from forty-eight students in mathematics and nine teachers of mathematics. The form and content of surveys and mathematical worksheets used is justified and detailed in the text of the research. The student's t-test was used in the analysis of two different populations with variances. The result of the study is that algebra relies strongly on abstract reasoning and structure sense. Geometry does not.

The Impact of Algebra vs. Geometry on a Learner's Ability to Develop Reasoning Skills

Students in the United States (U.S.) perform inadequately on state, national, and international standardized mathematics assessments (Polly, 2008). This is a major concern for all stakeholders in the educational community (Flores & Flores, 2008). The U.S. Department of Education (2008) reported only 23% of twelfth grade students in the nation are proficient in mathematics.

Statement of the Problem

U.S. educational reform efforts have consisted of school improvements that promote learning and higher levels of achievement (Fuhrman & Odden, 2001). Teachers traditionally enter the profession with idealistic motives, such as the desire to affect children; however, they must evolve to meet the challenges of changing educational demands that include high expectations of federal mandates, the increase of immigrant students with limited English, political and economic changes, and local school district expectations (Gregory & Chapman, 2007).

Darling-Hammond (2003) contended every reform effort has consisted of variation or creation of curriculum, assessment, programs, or school models. Scholars have begun to assert that the only way to facilitate improvement in schools is to improve teacher instruction (McCombs, Daniels, & Perry, 2008). The lack of achievement in schools has been largely attributed to poorly trained or unmotivated teachers (Zimmerman & Dibenedetto, 2008); however, empirical research has begun to illustrate that teachers' knowledge and pedagogical practices affect achievement for all students (Marzano, 2003).

Exposing students to excellent teaching is thought to bring about the change sought after by waves of unsuccessful reform since the 1950s (Mayrowetz, The Impact on Algebra vs. Geometry of a Learner's Ability to Develop Reasoning Skills

2009). Thus, effective or ineffective reform is largely dependent upon the knowledge base, instructional skills, and commitment of teachers (Darling Hammond, 2003). Lovat and Toomey (2009), suggested quality teaching has no singular definition, but generally refers to the juxtaposition of effective practices, delivery of content, and maintenance of a positive learning environment for students.

Educators and policymakers have historically not agreed on a mathematics curriculum or which kind of mathematics should be taught (Woodward, 2004). High school mathematics allows students to access a wide variety of career and educational opportunities (N C T M, 2004). The National Council of Teachers of Mathematics (NCTM) reported that an optimal mathematics experience involves intermixing algebra, geometry, statistics, probability, and discrete math. However, conflict has existed between supporters of traditional mathematics education and proponents of reform that came after the N C T M developed new standards in 1989 (Bodovski & Farkas, 2007).

Wilkins (2008) recognized the importance of the beliefs of a mathematics teacher and conducted a study that incorporated the additional variables of mathematical content knowledge, attitudes, and instructional practices into a study of 481 teachers. Teacher participants were selected from two rural southeastern school districts and surveyed using a 44-item TIMSS survey. Teacher attitudes regarding mathematics and teaching mathematics affected positively the frequency of use of research-based instructional practices. In contrast, teachers' mathematical content knowledge negatively affected use of research-based instructional practices. Wilkins also concluded that teacher beliefs had the strongest effect on instructional practices.

Teacher beliefs regarding the specific domains of mathematics, such as algebra and geometry, provide insight into teachers and instructional practices. A search of the literature for the present study revealed an incomplete and unbalanced body of knowledge involving teacher beliefs and problem solving. Nathan and Koedinger (2000) conducted a survey of 107 K-12 teachers of mathematics. Teachers were asked to rank tasks and respond to six different surveys about views of mathematics, instruction, and student learning. Researchers discovered teachers believed that students can problem-solve, multiple methods of algebraic problem solving exist, teachers should encourage students to invent methods of problem solving, and students should be evaluated based on conceptual understanding, not simply the final answer (Nathan & Koedinger, 2000).

On a larger scale, the Alabama Department of Education participated in a study of educators' perceptions of nine research-based educational strategies developed by Marzano (Pritchett & Black, 2009). Ninety-two percent of the participants were high school administrators with an average teaching experience of thirteen years. Four of Marzano's instructional practices were reported as used most often: homework, practice, reinforcing effort, and providing recognition. All nine research strategies were found to be "somewhat important" (p.140). Pritchett and Black (2009) concluded a significant correlation existed between implementation and perceived importance of instructional strategies; teachers perceived that student achievement was associated with use of research-based instructional strategies. Thompson (2004) reported that perceptions of mathematics may affect instructional practices; thus, research has sought to transform mathematics education by studying and changing teacher perceptions.

The high school of study failed to make Adequate Yearly Progress (AYP) since reporting began in the 2003-2004 school year, and more recently in the 2008-2009 school year. As a result, the district was assigned for the second time to the jurisdiction of the state, and all administrative staff of the school was fired. Fifty percent of the teachers were also fired. The superintendent for the district resigned. More specifically, Union High School is on the Needs Improvement List due to failure to meet the criteria for AYP in the 2008-2009 school year, according to the Tier Two Definition used by the state of California, which is waiting for federal acceptance of the new designation. To date, no studies have been conducted at Union High School investigating teacher perceptions and lived experiences of research-based mathematics instructional practices. The lack of research constitutes the gap in the knowledge upon which the study is based.

Statement of Purpose

The question being examined is whether or not Number Sense, Structure Sense, and Abstract Reasoning have a different impact on Algebra than they have on Geometry. One category of the subjects in this experiment, the teachers, arrives in the classroom with different levels of both ability and understanding of teaching and evaluating abstract reasoning as a skill (Quinn,1997). Thus, research in this area must continue and be incorporated into curriculum frameworks, state mathematics standards, and professional development (Hoch & Dreyfus, 2004), so that the other category of subjects in this experiment, the students (in this case forty-seven students total, a complete class on Algebra II students and Geometry students), might be able to acquire these skills.

Review of Literature

The following literature review is organized into five subtopics, with the first subtopic discussed, supporting the statement of the problem and statement of purpose. Also, there are Prevailing Definitions of Reasoning Skills, and Skills Evaluated or Taught, which, along with the next subtopic, Influence of Instructors' Backgrounds, Impact on Algebra vs. Geometry, narrows the field of study. Every attempt has been made to place an emphasis on clarity. The foundation of this paper is to acknowledge that everyone is not familiar with these reasoning skills.

Prevailing Definitions of Reasoning Skills

Number Sense is considered the first of all reasoning skills, according to Faulkner (2009). Researchers often define Number Sense from various points of views. Faulkner (2009) argued it is easier to examine practical work of both the instructor and the student to recognize Number Sense and then derive a working definition. Faulkner (2009) described the aspects of Number Sense as follows: fluency in estimating and judging magnitude; ability to recognize unreasonable results; flexibility when mentally computing; and ability to move among different representations and use the most appropriate representations. Faulkner (2009) also presented of the components of Number Sense as follows: algebraic and geometric thinking; proportional reasoning; language; form of a number; equality; base ten; numeration; and quantity magnitude. Curriculum and framework, in the form of standards, support the instructor in defining and focusing on Number Sense. This is often done through professional development courses or test questions found in standardized tests with remarks to the instructor that point out that the questions are based upon Number Sense (Faulkner, 2009).

The definition of Structure Sense is new in terms of the history of mathematics. This is according to the researchers who use it (Linchevski and Livnch, 1999). The high school student has Structure Sense if the following occurs: he or she can recognize a familiar structure in its simplest form; he or she can deal with a compound term as a single entity, and through an appropriate substitution, recognize a familiar structure in a more complex form {SS1 as abbreviated}; the Substitution Principle, an important aspect of Structure Sense, identifies the following concept: "If a parameter is replaced by a compound term (product, power, but no sum) {SS2a as abbreviated}, or a sum and possibly a product or power {SS2b as abbreviated}, or if a compound term is replaced by a parameter, the structure remains the same; and he or she can choose appropriate manipulations to make the best use of a structure {MS as abbreviated}. The structure is in simplest form (SS3 as abbreviated). The structure is in simplest form {SS3}. The compound structure has a product or power, but no sum {SS3a}. The compound structure contains a sum, but no power or product {SS3b}" (Hoch & Dreyfus, 2006, 2008).

Abstract Reasoning depends heavily upon the mastery of structure sense (Sfard & Linchevski, 1994). It is believed that this is difficult to quantify, define, evaluate and/or qualify properly, and is best explained if discussed as a transition from the operational to the structural, and then finally to the abstract. To make any sense of this, Sfard and Linchevski, (1994) suggested that operational and structural Algebra as generalized arithmetic and is not to be viewed as an increase in complexity and/ or sophistication. The actual move to the abstract is an increase in sophistication. As discussed later in this section, it becomes an immediately structural and graphic example of what might be diagrams and proofs. The example of this given by Sfard and Linchevski (1994) is that the major contributions for symbolization occurred in the sixteenth century when Francois Viete replaced numbers with symbols. Sfard and Linchevski's (1994), references pertaining to operational abstract algebra were first published in 1830 in Britain, and structural abstract algebra was contributed in the nineteenth century with group, rings, and field theory.

The dominate researchers in the area of reasoning skills are Maureen Hoch, Tommy Dreyfus, Jarmila Novotna, and Liora Linchevski, based on the validity and reliability of their theories, as performed by these dominant researchers. These researchers also have the most recent contributions in this area of research. The researchers used mixed methods (Hoch & Dreyfus,

2005). They designed pretests and posttests, and interviewed student subjects (Hoch & Dreyfus, 2007; Novotna & Hoch, 2008). Interviews were done with video tape and audio recorders first, before the students were deemed to be well versed in Algebra, and second, after the students appeared to be well versed in Algebra. In the second instance, the students were videotaped giving instruction to their peers (Sfard & Linchevski, 1994).

In most cases, the successful subjects displayed SS1 and SS2. Successful students did not often display MS when tested for it. Successful students displayed Number Sense to some degree, and Abstract reasoning to some degree. Evaluator recognition of all three reasoning skills is somewhat suspect (Steffe,1990). All successful subjects, students and instructors, used Number Sense, Structure Sense, and Abstract Reasoning. The presence of devices such as brackets helped in the calculations and led to more accuracy. Hoch et al. (2004) concluded an individual's attention can and must be drawn to structure.

There is a consensus that students need to be well versed in Number Sense and Structure Sense (Kamens, 1996). There were no conclusions to the contrary. This reviewer found nothing in the literature to the contrary of what was presented in this review. As publications of these researchers are reviewed, it is apparent that most of the issues are finitely defined. Paolo Boero (2001), for instance, works very closely with the strands of research that investigate mathematical language and symbolism in the classroom and clearly arrived at the opinion held by most of the researchers cited more prominently in the literature review. Throughout, the question remains: if reasoning skills can be identified and or defined, which can be universally taught or evaluated? Reys (1984) concluded most researchers have this concern.

Skills Evaluated or Taught

The primary concern of teachers, administrators, and school district curriculum coordinators is if these skills can be evaluated and taught. The support for the position that these skills can be taught by teachers and other auxiliary personnel is that there is a structure in place for educating and evaluating instructors about these reasoning skills, and standards, frameworks, professional development, and other consistent methods are in place to monitor both the students and instructors (Cooney, 1999; Reys, 1984). Izsak (2000) argued there is the more obvious proof that children do go to school and try to accomplish tasks that cannot be performed without these skills. Yet, concern has been constantly raised by researchers about the issue of mastery of these reasoning skills by both the student and instructor, and this concern may contribute to any final success gained by the student and/or the instructor (Faulkner, 2009; Goodson-E spy, 1998; Reys, et al., 2003).

Sfard and Linchevski (1994) are strong sources of information in this area. Research has shown they have been cited at least once in most papers in the area of student and instructor ability to demonstrate some area structure sense and/or abstract reasoning (Ferrari, 2003; Hazzan & Zazkis, 2005; Van Dooren, Verschaffel, & Onghena, 2002). Sfard and Linchevski (1994) used charting tools, interviews, and videotaped interviews to prepare problems and implement monitoring for further evaluations. The charting technique, for instance, was used to bring the mind of the subject through abstraction to a concrete position.

Sfard and Linchevski (1994) used proofs in tabular form to do a timeline to support their reasoning with regard to the development or recognition of Structure Sense and/ or Abstract Reasoning. Sfard and Linchevski (1994) used both a historical and a psychological perspective to substantiate their view of the development of Algebraic thinking. Their approaches were used on groups into which the student subjects had been divided. They discussed the Israeli approach to teaching Algebra, which is interesting because the first set of dominate researchers in the area, Hoch and Dreyfus, were teaching in Israel. T ere is an unstated or understated shift toward Israeli techniques in teaching Algebra and/ or Geometry.

Sfard and Linchevski's (1994) approach mentioned above is shown in publications in tabular form. In their interviews of student subjects, the researchers clarified the student approach to Algebra (Dole, 2003). Sfard and Linchevski (1994) concluded that students do not want to find any answers that do not lead them to standard or well-known algorithms. They do not want to discover their own laws or theorems. Therefore, their developmental model, which has led to a new finding, is at odds with any structural approach to teaching Algebra. The student can and will always become more comfortable with the operational approach and try to avoid the structural approach.

In summary, researchers cited in previous paragraphs suggest that the student must somehow arrive at Structure Sense and Abstract Reasoning. If the student does master Structure Sense, he or she will have more correct, more accurate solutions to their work. This, together with Abstract Reasoning, should lead the student to more understanding as well (Sfard, et al., 1994).

If Sfard and Linchevski (1994) are right, there is an extant question about whether educators are equipped to provide the guidance that children need. There also remains the question about whether this can be monitored—in both the students and the teachers—without becoming burdensome to both. Is the existing focus on teaching these skills enough to prepare every child for college and/ or the real world?

Influence of Instructor's Background

Instructor knowledge in any subject influences the performance of the student (Van Dooren, et al., 2002). A way to approach the issue of instructor competency is to take a detailed look at standardized tests, such as the SAT and others. Most such test providers do not have a statistical sampling or the expertise needed to be considered valid researchers. The Sebrecht group does have such expertise (Sebrecht, Enright, Bennet, & Martin, 1996).

Another approach might be to look at the states with the best schools in the U.S., as did the White group (White, Gamoran, Smithson, & Porter, 1996). Those states are the state of California and the state of New York. Educators are good at policing their own house;

thus, there is no dominate researcher in this area. An examination of curricula and standards would provide information, particularly if gathered from other countries as well as the U.S. (Kamens, et al. 1996; Reys, et al., 2003).

Responsibility for the end result is not something that the instructor can avoid. What does really happen when the instructor is teaching out if his or her area of knowledge? The student is unhappy, the teacher is unhappy, and both sides manifest anger. It is no longer a learning situation. As hard as the student tries to learn and the teacher tries to teach, this situation should be interrupted immediately, for neither party is accomplishing a positive result (Cooney, 1996; Steffe, 1990; Van Dooren, et al., 2002).

Van Dooren, et al. (2002) circulated a questionnaire focused upon the effect of teacher knowledge on assessing student work and teaching. The questionnaire was comprised of six word problems. One question was arithmetic and one was algebraic. The solution was graded with ten points. The ninety-seven teacher participants were told that ninth graders did the problems, and that the solutions would be graded (a) algebraically, (b) arithmetically—manipulate the structure, and (c) arithmetically—guess and check.

The researchers observed the way each teacher proposed the solution to the problems. They believed it would influence grading, and the results proved this to be the case. Results were presented in an easy-to-read tabular format, often using AN O VA. In addition, subjects were asked why they thought they did what they did, but their answers did not influence the conclusions of the researchers, who felt most of their hypothetical positions had been supported.

The conclusion of these researchers was also based on a questionnaire. The researchers demonstrated their attempts to deliver accurate unbiased results and conclusions. When all facts were analyzed and viewed from the unbiased position of statistical significance, it was concluded there was a need for further investigation into the abilities and attitudes of in-class mathematics instructors. There was no conclusion to the contrary to be found in the searched literature either located by this researcher or referenced by anyone else.

This must be a challenging subject, or at the very least, a "touchy" subject. These researchers implied that it must be addressed.

There are no real remaining issues to be addressed except clarifying or bringing more evidence to support or denounce existing positions. It is important to keep a focus on the real questions and issues. The next section is offered by way of doing just that and in summation.

Impact on Algebra vs. Geometry

No researcher in the surveyed twenty-five year time period were willing to continue research into the impact of Algebra versus Geometry, other than that Algebra moves almost immediately to abstraction, and Geometry stays in a more concrete realm. Both Algebra and Geometry both benefit by having the students possess skills in Number Sense and Structure Sense. Number Sense only is present in the State of California's curricula as a standard. The presence in the standards indicates agreement not presented here because it would dominate the literature review.

The dominant researchers in this area are Sfard and Linchevski (1994), who, in their thoroughness, touched upon this issue, as they did both a current and historical review of abstract Algebra. The researchers support their position by using math historians, as well as techniques and conclusion drawn historically from mathematicians long ago. They use an excellent reasoning process as the build of the concept of operational and structural abstract Algebra. The unchallenged statement is made that operational Algebra precedes structural Algebra.

In an attempt to recognize the attributes or reasoning skills, three groups of four children, aged 12-13, 14-15, and 15-16, were taught an equation and asked to explain it to their peers. This technique was used to obtain a certain result from the students. It was thought to give a more honest representation of what was happening than direct questioning. Results were videotaped. When a student could not explain the whole scenario, it was deemed that the student could not make the transition from Number Sense to Structure Sense.

The researchers said they concluded that the operational skills were basic, but the structural skill was developmental. They also clarified that both are needed for Algebra and Geometry, and that both are needed to proceed to abstract reasoning. As long as the equation looks arithmetical, when the unknown is only on one side, the child will at least try to solve it and can usually solve it.

There seem to be no conclusions to the contrary. In fact, the researchers themselves call the recognition of this problem on the part of qualified instructor observers elusive at best. They strongly imply that this should be brought to the attention of their peers. The author of the present study concurs. For want of a better expression, anything that is scientifically reproducible and causes no harm to the subject should be explored. This is sensitive subject in the field of Mathematics. Misconceptions about what the student is thinking prevail.

Summary

Number Sense, Structure Sense, and Abstract Reasoning are an important aspect of learning and teaching Mathematics (Falkner, 2009). What no researcher has suggested is that a student with a reasonable Algebraic background not doing well in the more abstract parts of Algebra might do quite well in most parts of Geometry in a high school setting. Should this be the case, the instructor should do his or her part so that the child can be successfully supported and provided with the confidence to accomplish the tasks they understand (Falkner, 2009). The instructor must at all times stay competent so there are no attitudinal presentations on either side (Quinn, 1997). No classroom is perfect, but by staying on top of his or her circumstances, whatever they may be, the instructor must be true to the subject matter, themselves, and the students (Falkner, 2009).

Some researchers feel that these findings affect the curricula needed.

Teachers should push for these concepts to appear in state math frameworks. The National Council of Teachers of Mathematics was willing to publish these ideas in their publications (Van Dooren, et al., 2002). Maybe they do more. Learned and often tenured groups like these seem to want to do more.

California is a good example of a progressive curriculum (White, 1996). Yet, the answer might be no to all of the above questions. If people who make changes understand these issues, would those changes be made? It is highly likely that these issues are not thoroughly understood (Steffe, 1990). Mandatory professional development, and help of the Internet, may highlight these issues. Change will happen if instructors are not allowed to work out of their content area. Leaders must also be willing to change.

Defining the various aspects of Structure Sense is a new direction (Hoch & Dreyfus, 2007). This is also a positive direction for research and application in the classroom. The researchers, having addressed the complexities involved in the classroom, have taken the first step to solving some of the problems (Steffe, 1990). The need for the basic reasoning skills and the impact of Algebra or Geometry will intensify as technology makes it harder to make a mistake in calculations and/ or drawing to scale. This will show the reasoning of the student when assessing or evaluating assigned activities (Kamens, 1996).

The following section is a summary of the methods used to explore the contrasts and comparisons between three reasoning skills used in Algebra and Geometry at Union High School in Northern California. The present study was designed to investigate teacher perceptions of research-based instructional practices. As well, the design was an effort to discover the research-based instructional practices most utilized by teachers in the Algebra and Geometry curriculum.

Methods

The methods used and results of this mostly quantitative methods research may provide clarity that will result in increased levels of teacher and student performance when applied to the teaching of mathematics. Clear and concise definitions of number sense structure sense and abstract reasoning can be introduced into teacher professional development forums and ultimately in the classroom, based on results of the study. The following section summarizes the setting and participants, procedure, and data analysis of the study.

Participants

Participants were teachers or students at a secondary Title One school entitled Union High School (pseudonym). Title One schools are schools that failed to make Adequate Yearly Progress (AYP) as defined by the No Child Left Behind Act. The lower- to middle-class school district where the study was undertaken is forty-five years old and has been taken over at least once in the last five years by the State of California for not making AYP. The current decision of the state is to take this district over again and let go a number of staff and principals. The teachers held a union-led strike in the last two years before the beginning of standardized testing conducted yearly by the state. Tensions are currently high in this well-integrated school system that has a large portion of Hispanic bilingual, Black, and Asian students, but not because of racial issues, but because of the need for adequate pay and good test scores.

Participants were teachers from the school's Math Department, and students in one Algebra I/ II class and one Geometry class. Each class had 2127 students, and there were nine teachers who had contact with one or another of these students during the class. This was a total of 110 faculty and student participants. Algebra I is a requirement for graduation in California schools.

Materials

The principal and the district allowed the researcher full access to the information relevant to the instructor's education and background (Appendix C). The principal and the district allowed access to the student files and pertinent records as was done with the instructors. Where there was any confusion, the researcher double checked with the campus data office.

The students were given three math worksheets (instruments) at different times during the first quarter of the school year. Students were instructed to complete them to the best of their ability and to show their work. The students used number two pencils. The instrument, in the case of Structure Sense, was constructed by the researcher based on the definitions given by Hoch and Dreyfus (2006). Hoch and Dreyfus (2006) based their work on Linchevski and Livneh (1999).

There were fifteen dichotomous question surveys for instructors and four constructed response question handouts for the students, along with observation sheets for researcher eyes only. Consent forms were acquired from the students and teachers (Appendix B). Survey Monkey was used to construct, distribute, and tabulate the instructor surveys. This researcher created the surveys. Minitab, a computer program, was also needed. All worksheets and other paper goods were produced using a standard computer, Microsoft Office, and various copy machines.

Procedure

The nine teachers were given a simple fifteen dichotomous/open-ended questions that were comprised of multiple choice questions relative to the reasoning skills of number sense, structure sense, and abstract reasoning. The questions posed had to be answered with "yes," "no," or "other and explain," which meant explain your choice. All teachers answered the questions and were not alienated by the procedures being used. This was important because it was the best way to proceed to the next step, which was student interaction. To avoid any sign of bias, this information was collected but not viewed until after all other experimental data was collected.

Students were given three math worksheets at different times during the first quarter of the school year (they can be found in the appendices of this document) and told to complete them to the best of their ability and show their work. Data was collected from the students at the time their curriculum was presented. For instance, information on structure sense was collected before difference of squares was taught and after difference of squares was taught. The abstract reasoning observation was continuous. The student files as mentioned in the methods section were also viewed after the quarter was over, and the respective school counselors, who were The Impact on Algebra vs. Geometry of a Learner's Ability to Develop Reasoning Skills

assigned to the students alphabetically by last name, were given an opportunity to have input.

Instructor's appointments were made for interviews at a mutually agreeable place and time with each participant. Appointments were made for one hour, with the caveat that a follow-up interview might be required to clarify any ambiguous or confusing data. To begin the interview, participants were reminded of the confidentiality of participation and asked to reread the letter of invitation and review the consent form. Participants were reminded that participation was voluntarily, and the decision to withdraw had no penalty. Confidentiality was assured.

Interviews were held prior to teachers answering the surveys on their own computers. Teachers were told they were free to use any reference materials needed to answer the questions. If they were to acknowledge Structure Sense and Abstract Reasoning as being located in something they routinely referenced, it would constitute a significant finding. The premise of the present study was that these terms, used in this context, were unfamiliar or only vaguely familiar to teachers, as in the case of Abstract Reasoning.

Qualitative data consisted of participants' perceptions and lived experiences, which was obtained through the interviews. In a qualitative study, comprising of interviews, "the participants must be individuals who have all experienced the phenomenon being explored and can articulate their lived experiences" (Creswell, 2009, p 119). The purpose of the interviews was to obtain raw data from candid individuals who were willing to share lived experiences of the phenomenon under study.

Following the recommendations of Rubin and Rubin (2005), some standardized sets of interview questions were asked of the instructors who met the inclusion criteria. Interviews were comprehensive and field notes were taken to assist the investigator in the interpretation of the underlying concepts. Interviews were transcribed verbatim from field notes.

The students were given three math worksheets (instruments) at different times during the first quarter of the school year (Appendix E). Students were instructed to complete them to the best of their ability. They were told that it was imperative that they show their work.

The worksheet was evaluated by the researcher using the following criteria.

SurveyMonkey and Excel were used to analyze data after application of the instrument. Worksheets were reviewed, and it was determined what Structure Sense, if any, was being displayed by the approach that was taken to solve the problem, to include minor mistakes such as misplaced negative signs or addition errors, which were ignored. The student had to show the work in such a manner that it would be clear they were trying to work with a sum or difference of squares, for instance, or that they were making a clear substitution after recognizing the nature of the structure.

Because the first stage of this complicated process was "recognition," participants were observed until it was obvious that recognition had been achieved (Cifarelli, 1988). Some participants arrived at this point only by listening to the instructor, some heard other classroom comments, and some were told verbally. It was recognition that was chosen for measurement, and this information was entered in the analysis section of SurveyMonkey. All participants and their answers were color-coded. This information was processed through SurveyMonkey, where it was response-base filtered and cross tabulated. In addition, the tallied section and chart section was used for analysis (SurveyMonkey, 2010). An instructor's demographic information and cumulative files for students were coded by color and analyzed by comparison in SurveyMonkey bar graphs. It was discovered that cross tabulation was not useful even though the instructor survey cross tabulations are presented for the reader to peruse. The researcher, based upon the advice of D r. E ric Seuss, Chair of the California State University of the East Bay's recommendation, that a t test be used for the student data (personal communication December 2, 2010 and forward). The information was input into Excel using standard two populations with unequal numbers and variance statistical formulas. Dr. Seuss was able to verify using Minitab ("Minitab," 2011; "Student's t-test," 2011). Calculations were checked and double checked until the researcher was satisfied as to the results.

A worksheet was constructed, combining the techniques of Hoch and Dreyfus (2005; 2007; 2006; 2004). The worksheet required a no-penalty written response to exercises commonly believed to demonstrate proficiency in structure sense. All students were offered extra credit for completion and doing the best job. The evaluation of the student's all-around abstract reasoning abilities was conducted through observation of selected lectures and assignments. The observer closely watched the students to ascertain the first moment when the student recognized the issues in the fashion recommended by Hennigsen and Stein (1997). Even if the student did not participate by raising his or her hand or answering aloud, there would be signs of recognition in facial expressions or body language.

Data Analysis

One of the five strands that are the organizing units of the California Mathematics Standards is Number Sense. Number Sense is referred to nine times in the Standards. Number Sense is clearly described and taught in professional development classes (Phillip Gonzalves' Summer Institute for Math Teachers, July 2008). A search of the Standards and the Framework revealed that Structure Sense and Abstract Reasoning are omitted from the discourse; yet, Number Sense is considered foundational to the other two reasoning skills.

Students display Structure Sense in high school Algebra if they can recognize a familiar structure in its simplest form (SSI). Students also need to be able to deal with a compound term as a single entity, and through appropriate substitution, recognize a familiar structure in a more complex form (SSII), where the compound term contains a product or power, but no sum, and where the compound term contains a sum and possibly a product or power. The student also needs to be able to choose appropriate manipulations to make best use of a structure (SSIII). This structure is in its simplest form. Further, the compound term contains a product or power.

Following the recommendations of Rubin and Rubin (2005), some standardized sets of interview questions were asked of nine math instructors who met the inclusion criteria. Interviews were comprehensive and field notes were taken to assist the investigator in the interpretation of the underlying concepts. Interviews were transcribed verbatim from field notes. After transcription was complete, data coding and analysis was conducted. Thematic analysis was implemented to identify the primary themes emerging from the interviews. The central themes described the math instructor's experiences with the phenomenon under study.

Line-by-line coding of the transcripts was the first stage in the analysis process. Initial descriptive coding, using the words or phrases of the participants, involved looking for repetition within and across the transcripts (Rubin & Rubin, 2005). After the coding process was completed for each individual transcript, the list of codes was examined to identify common concepts. Similar code terms and phrases were grouped together and then regrouped to include all of the identified concepts into categories of similar topics. Redundant codes and concepts were discarded. Looking for relationships, the categories were re-sorted into groups of similar content and meaning.

The investigator identified dominant categories by recognizing code words or phrases consistently repeated within and across the transcripts. The categories were further reviewed, paying particular attention to similarities and differences in the responses to the interview questions. Finally, themes were identified by reviewing and organizing the categories into common topics. The themes were refined through several reviews of the transcripts.

The worksheet was evaluated by the researcher using the following criteria.

SurveyMonkey was used to analyze data after application of the instrument. Worksheets were reviewed, and it was determined what Structure Sense, if any, was displayed by the approach that was taken to solve the problem, to include minor mistakes such as misplaced negative signs or addition errors, which were ignored. The student had to show the work in such a manner that it would be clear they were trying to work with a sum or difference of squares, for instance, or that they were making a clear substitution after recognizing the nature of the structure.

Because the first stage of this complicated process was "recognition," participants were observed until it was obvious that recognition had been achieved (Cifarelli, 1988). Some participants arrived at this point only by listening to the instructor, some heard other classroom comments, and some were told verbally. Recognition was chosen for measurement, and this information was entered in the analysis section of SurveyMonkey. All participants and their answers were color-coded. This information was processed through SurveyMonkey, where it was response-base filtered and cross tabulated. In addition, the tallied section and chart section was used for analysis (SurveyMonkey, 2010).

Instructor demographic information and cumulative files for students were coded by color and analyzed by comparison in SurveyMonkey bar graphs.

Findings

The findings may well show that the follow-up interviews to the survey results brought some much-needed clarification to the results as to actually seem contradictory. Eight of the nine teachers in the Mathematics department took the survey and participated willingly in the follow-up interviews. The ninth instructor, even though the study was authorized by her principal, chose not to participate. This is a very realistic situation and does show the pressures on the teachers in a Title One school to put their best foot forward or to conform to what they believed to be the status quo when talking to the researcher. In the analysis of the data, the following subtopics emerged: teaching practices, evaluating practices, and teaching and math department perceptions.

Teaching Practices

One of the five strands that are the organizing units of the California Mathematics Standards is Number Sense. Number Sense is referred to no less than nine times in as many sections of this document: pages 8; 10; 13; 20; 24; 29; 33; and 38. Number Sense is then clearly described and taught in professional development, and because of the Williams Act has to be available to the parents and students. When using the traditional lesson plans, the standards must be explained to the students at the beginning of the lecture. A search of that same document will tell one that Structure Sense and Abstract Reasoning are not included in this document. Things worsen if Number Sense is considered foundational to the other two reasoning skills. Research in this area is needed.

Perhaps even content area research should be mandatory and incorporated into Professional Development. This researcher found that there was an obvious discomfort amongst the teachers at Union High School, who did willingly participate in this study that seemed to be based on their view of themselves as uninformed and, in many ways, obsolete. The follow-up interviews soundly established that the teachers actually did not know anything about any of these reasoning skills other than Number Sense. They all stated this many times verbally. The interviews were written down and weighted for its incorporation into this report. It was found or decided that it had to consider the truer and more accurate findings relative to the survey even though the charts only analyze the surveys. Just being a member of organizations like NT C M and taking a magazine or two does not seem to be a confidence builder, because, in my findings with this group of subjects, it was true they were members of various associations but still displayed the signs of lack of confidence to the point that the survey answers contradicted the follow-up interview answers.

Survey Monkey was used to evaluate the suspicion of this researcher that it was common for a teacher to stay up-to-date in this fashion, meaning that they would always tend to rely heavily on some sort of Professional Development and Professional convention seminars to keep informed. To gather this information, the researcher constructed a dichotomous/open-ended survey. There is an urgent need for this type of analysis, as well as the principal's assisted review of the teachers' educational backgrounds. The Mathematics Department felt confident, after taking the survey, and much discussion about whether or not all were trained to evaluate Number Sense as it was spelled out in the California Mathematics Framework and Standards, that although the students had not made adequate yearly progress, which is below the performance of any average student by definition, the other subjects, the teachers, were demonstrative of their population. The researcher was careful to take any comment or suggestion relative to what was actually the status quo.

The principal, who was actually hired by the state, as a consequence of the fact that his predecessors failed to lead the campus through to adequate yearly progress, was, by virtue of his experience, an invaluable source of information. The teachers who would give information, and this was the case with all of them, were extremely lucid with regards to their own performance and the performance of their peers. Again it is to be understood that the teachers all had greater than eleven years in classroom experience.

It was in the follow-up interview that it was discovered that due to the Title One, Tier Two classification, the teachers gave misleading answers. This was easier to ascertain because this researcher opened all interviews with a question or a reminder that all surveys could be answered open book or open Internet. Any reminder of the open book format of the survey put the teachers at ease during the follow-up interview. The teachers could say clearly that they could not locate any reference material with regards to Structure Sense and were not that comfortable with Abstract Reasoning. It is their practice, the majority insisted, to be extremely familiar with the State Standards and Mathematic Framework as the Williams Act, District, State, and No Child Left Behind Law require.

Evaluating Practices

A student, one of our subjects, is said to display Structure Sense for high school Algebra if he or she can recognize a familiar structure in its simplest form (SSI) and deal with a compound term as a single entity and through appropriate substitution recognize a familiar structure in a more complex form (SSII), i.e., where the compound term contains a product or power but no sum, or where the compound term contains a sum and possibly also a product or power. Also, a student displays Structure Sense if they choose appropriate manipulations to make best use of a structure (SSIII) where the structure is in its simplest form, the compound term contains a product or power but no sum, or the compound term contains a sum and possibly also a product or power. The researcher reviewed the worksheets and determined what Structure Sense, if any, was being displayed.

The definition of abstract reasoning must be addressed before the concept can be analyzed, and therefore evaluated, as was done in the Literature Review. Paraphrased, abstract reasoning means the quality of relationships between the object of thought and the thinking person, a reflection of the process, and the complexity of the concept of thought. The Number Sense observations were done along with the abstract reasoning observations and will be discussed at that time. The structure sense findings support the hypothesis because this information could not be cross tabulated as was originally proposed in the Methods section. A standard hypothesis based on the Ho and Ha was used. It is to be remembered that H o is the status quo and that H a is the other alternative, when looking at statistical significance.

H o: Algebra II students are no more adept at structure sense than Geometry students and will perform no better and with no more or less accuracy on any problem where Structure Sense is foundational.

H a: Algebra II students are more adept than Geometry students and will perform better on any problem where Structure Sense is foundational.

These problems are found in both Algebra II and Geometry. The problems on the worksheet that were given to students in both classes were analyzed using the students' t test for two populations with unequal numbers and unequal variances. Variances are the measure of the spread of the numbers. The Algebra population sample size was twenty one and the Geometry population sample size was twenty seven. The variance for Algebra using standard statistical formulation found in Wikipedia on the Internet was 3.8809 and the variance for Geometry was 0.9409 using the same. The "t" statistic was 2.16 with 27 degrees of freedom. A "p" value of .02 was also calculated. The "p" value of .02 is less than the alpha of .05, the alpha level is the upper boundary of the type I errors; thus, H o is rejected. This was verified by Minitab and the Excel workbook is in the appendices.

The evaluation for the other category of subjects, the teachers, is more strenuous than the yearly review that might have been based on student test scores and in room observation, if there is no really adverse situation existing like in this case of inadequate yearly progress of the students. In this case, the entire faculty actually had to be terminated by the state and rehired by the new principal, who also was hired by the state to replace the existing administrative staff. This principal only had the option of rehiring fifty percent of the existing staff. When a Tier Two designation is given by the state, the existing staff is called into a large public meeting along with the community and parents to select one of four options. They are as follows: close the school; use the fifty percent rehire model described above; reorganize both students and teacher using a set formula (this means that the students may also be bused to other schools and even to other districts); and another hybrid of these options.

There was a large amount of written materials distributed to everyone at the meeting, which is another Williams Act mandate. This material described the schools affected and the four options and all time periods involved. As an example of the seriousness of the state, a school only a year and a half old, a brand new school, was on the list for closure. Each teacher from one of the subject schools, who seriously wants to remain in the district, must select or recommend one of these plans and explain why they think that it will work and submit by the end of this group of meetings, which takes place over about a two- to three-week time period. This researcher was present at two of the three meetings.

It could only be found that there was an obvious discrepancy between the Survey data and the Interview data. When asked why they had not been as clear as they could be on the survey questions, they all made some kind of clear reference to the "pressure" they were under because of the failure of the school in general and their classes in particular to reach satisfactory academic performance. It was clear that these teachers had passed their ultimate evaluation and were still employed

Teacher and Math Department Perceptions

Number Sense was observed and recorded by tally and recognition, as was abstract reasoning. Number Sense was consistently demonstrated by all students in the opinion of the researcher and all but the single teacher who refused all participation and showed only consistent unprovoked or solicited hostility. All participant instructors felt very confident with all aspects of recognition of Number Sense as was demonstrated in the answers to the survey questions and the follow-up interviews. All instructors related having greater than eleven years' experience in the classroom.

There was also a strong confidence level for abstract reasoning, but not so for Structure Sense. All eight remaining teachers had to be put at ease and admitted that they knew nothing about Structure Sense in both the survey and the follow-up interviews. The first chart displays the results obtained from the survey question, "Can you Define Structure Sense?" There are three bars on a horizontal bar graph, with two of the bars which represent a dichotomous yes/no section and an explanatory question that refers to whether or not a textbook or other reference was used to answer the question.

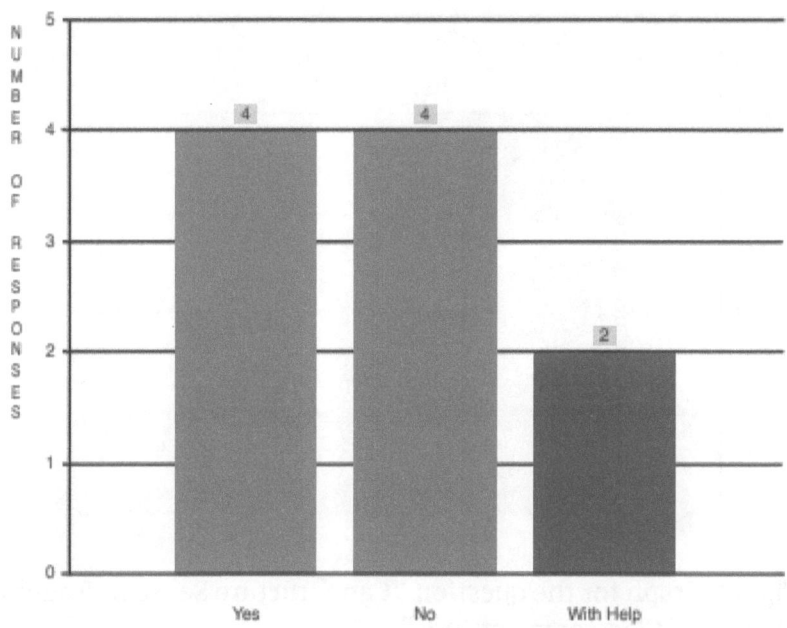

Fig. 1.1 Graph for the question "Can you define Structure Sense?"

Figure 1.1 demonstrates bar charts of the survey question "Can you define Structure Sense?" As one proceeds through the charts in this report, you can tell that the instructors display lack of confidence in their answers as if they do not know or are unsure. Instead of a simple yes, there are many more no answers then was in keeping with the flow of what any observer might reasonably expect and some who would need help from at least one textbook. For instance, the response to this question, a question about understanding the definition of something that needs to follow, actually determines how the answers must go for the questions that follow. As you will see, it did not. This needs to be brought to the reader's attention. One should note also that the answers in Fig. 1.2 show ten responses when only eight are possible. This error could not be removed from SurveyMonkey even when their technical support was employed to assist this researcher. The determination was made that this material was too valuable not to be presented to the reader and to assist any other researcher that might be interested in this subject.

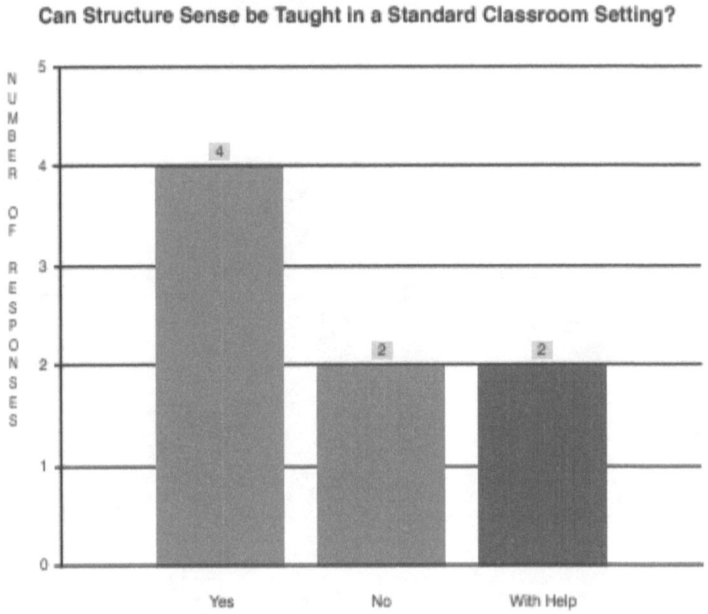

Can Structure Sense be Taught in a Standard Classroom Setting?

[Bar graph showing: Yes = 4, No = 2, With Help = 2. Y-axis: NUMBER OF RESPONSES, ranging 0 to 5.]

Fig. 1.2 Graph for the question "Can Structure Sense Be Taught in a Standard Classroom Setting?"

Fig.1.2. This chart is asking whether or not Structure Sense can be taught in a classroom setting versus something like a computer laboratory or any other setting (a computer laboratory was not actually written as an example on the survey, but there was no issue or confusion raised by the subjects.). To answer this question, the instructor must know the definition of Structure Sense and theoretically have used it and be able to answer how they acquired it or how they learned it.

Can Some Aspects of the Learned Structure Sense Be Evaluated in a Standard Classroom by an Instructor?

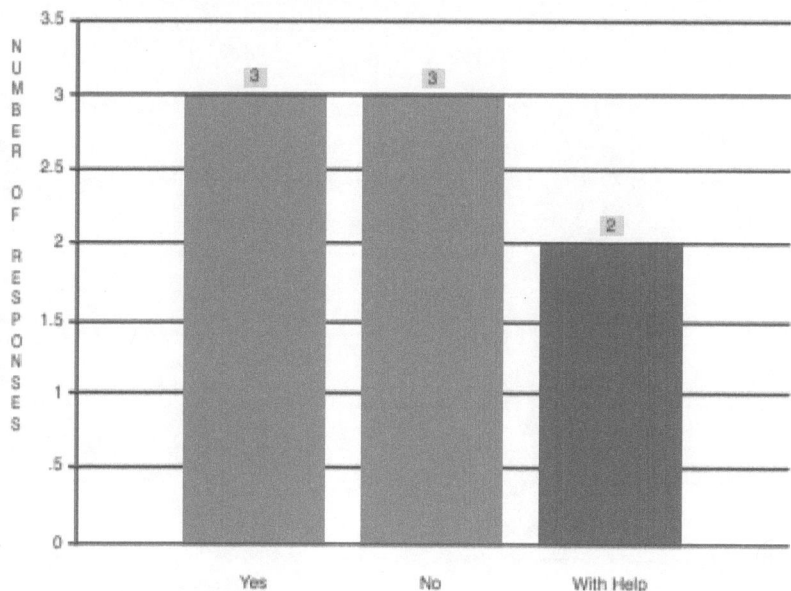

Fig. 1.3 Graph for the question "Can Some Aspects of the Learned Structure Sense Be Evaluated in a Standard Classroom by an Instructor?"

Fig. 1.3. The graph which depicts the results of the question "Can some aspects of learned Structure Senses be evaluated in a standard classroom by the instructor?" posed to the nine Math teachers. Like all the rest, there is a dichotomous yes/ no answer and the "with help like a textbook" answer. There was an even, or fifty-fifty, response to the dichotomous question. One would think that the "no" answer was extremely significant until the follow-up interviews explain this.

Where Did You Learn about Structure Sense? Check all that apply.

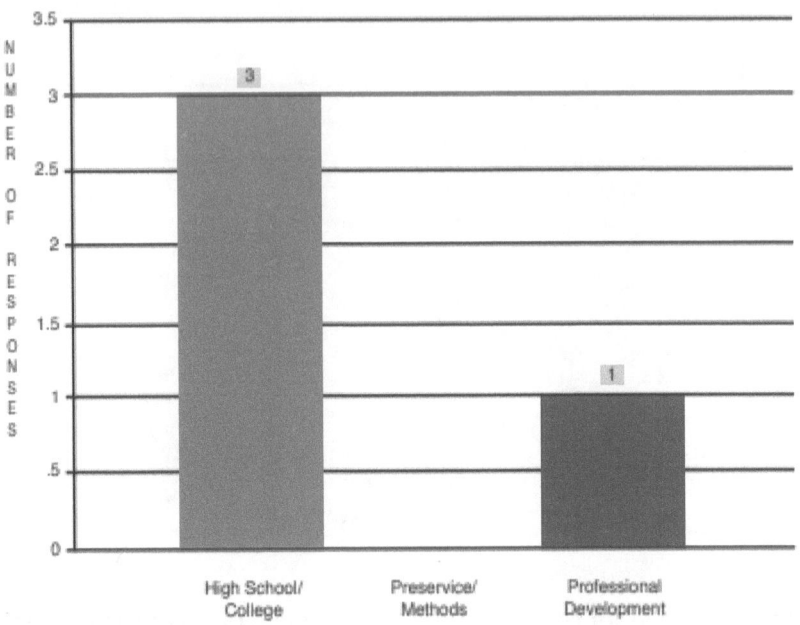

Fig. 1.4. This is the graph of the question "Where Did You Learn about Structure Sense?"

Fig.1.4. The graph of the question "Where did you learn about Structure Sense?" posed to the nine Math teachers. Note that only four teachers answered this question.

Finally, when asked where they learned about the skill, some instructors did not answer at all. (See figure 1.4.) During the follow-up interview they all admitted they were very unsure about Structure Sense and had no familiarity with it. They tried to look it up and could not find it anywhere. They also could not liken it to anything they were familiar with.

The observations made independently by the researcher showed that the

Algebra II students who were observed being lectured on Completing the Square, The Quadratic Formula, and Complex Conjugates, handled abstract concepts very well and were not overly challenged, whereas the Geometry students who were being lectured on the days/hours, Mid-segment theorem, and perpendicular bisector theorem, while other ideas were being touched upon, i.e., the Pythagorean Theorem, rushed to draw diagrams for the instructor. They made every attempt to move to the concrete aspect of any proof placed before them immediately.

Limitations

If it is indeed the case that abstraction is merely observing the student moving backward and forward from the concrete to the abstract, then the analysis is dependent upon the accuracy of this observation. This is often done in Geometry as a proof. Any "mental" math problem is solved by placing it back and forth from concrete to abstraction. A measure of reification is being called for, "the stage when the solver can conceive of the mathematical concept as complete object with characteristics of its own" (Goodson-E spy, 1998, p.191). Because the first stage of this complicated process is "recognition," the observer watched the participants until she was sure that the recognition had been arrived at during a lecture where higher thinking was taking place (Cifarelli, 1988). Some participants could arrive at this point only by listening to the instructor, some heard other classroom comments, and some were told verbally. It is recognition that has been chosen for measurement, and this information was put in the tally mark analysis section of SurveyMonkey.

The more obvious limitations were that the information was collected before the Thanksgiving holiday, when the students and the teachers were very tired from other obligations they had to meet during the quarter. There was a tendency for the students to say that they just wanted to get to the Thanksgiving break. This school was also under the direct authority of the state for the second time. Therefore, this is not a generalizable study.

Conclusion

Fortunately this research did culminate in a clear and concise quantitative conclusion. In spite of the fact that there was a large qualitative component to this investigation, the survey question format and the worksheet evaluation proved quite helpful in illuminating the issues to be found in this investigation. It was simple in concept and appearance.

Teaching Practices

Having discussed the limitations of this research, conclusions must be wrought carefully. The teachers freely admitted that they never heard of anything other than Number Sense and that they did not feel very comfortable with that one. It is not reasonable for a teacher who has been actively practicing their profession more than eleven years, as these teachers have been, to redo a methods course. However, that is considered the more viable solution by researchers in this field, unless professional development courses really correct this issue (Quinn 1997). This discomfort could be possibly alleviated if professional development encouraged or fostered a review of current literature, i.e., peer reviewed articles. It is therefore to be concluded that they could not be sure when they had taught any of the reasoning skills (Steffe, 1990). One is forced to conclude that none of the skills had actually been taught directly and analyzing these issues for indirect teaching components is beyond the scope of this paper. However, the differences found between the Algebra II students and the Geometry students cannot be ignored. The students are picking up some of the needed skills in Algebra II. The teachers are at a loss as to the reason why. Even when attempting re-teaching, a very large part of any teacher's tool box, they are not sure what to emphasize (Lalley and Miller, 2006). Lalley and Miller's (2006), not included in the literature review because they would have expanded the topic, findings support this researcher's findings in that re-teaching is one of the most successful ways of helping the students actually learn the material.

Evaluating Practices

It would appear that, at the very least, the topic undertaken was challenging and continues to challenge other researchers (Hoch &

Dreyfus, 2007). It has, however, been given a fair examination. This researcher feels comfortable saying that for the now, the testing approach is the best to date, and it can be said that by using these methods, the instructor can both teach and evaluate the subject reasoning skills. The worksheet itself has been indirectly the contributions of at least eleven research trials (Boero, 2001; Dreyfus and Eisenberg, 1996; Hoch 2003; Hoch and Dreyfus, 2004, 2005, 2006, 2007;

Linchevski and Livneh, 1999; Pierce and Stacey, 2001; Sfard and Linchevski, 1994; Novotna and Hoch, 2008). It is to be recalled that most of those researchers were heavily dependent upon the actual problem selection, like those in the worksheet.

It may also be proper to state that these approaches are ready to be examined under the lens of curriculum and professional development. They strongly tie into the findings of the researchers mentioned in the Literature Review. A good example is the recognition factor evaluated by using facial expressions on the students recorded on the tally sheet. This is straight out of Sfard & Linchevski (1994) in the Literature Review. Structure Sense is invaluable in giving students more accuracy in their answers and therefore more confidence. There was not a large selection here as far as number of subjects, but most of the direct instruction, by way of classroom lectures witnessed by this researcher, will place the students closer to Structure Sense in Algebra II than Geometry. The changes that have to be made need to be made from the top down or from the grassroots up. It will probably occur both ways. The teachers involved in the research have already made some waves with their administration in an attempt to better understand these reasoning skills.

Teacher and Math Department Perceptions

Finally, Algebra does call for more abstract reasoning than Geometry, and one might monitor this by recognition approaches as was suggested in the Literature Review. Teachers now only need to use the skills they already have been trained to use. They must observe their students when it is agreed upon between themselves and their Math Department what they are in fact trying to observe.

It is not to be forgotten that these teachers and their administration were amicable because they had already been notified that they had done so poorly in their testing that they had already been taken over by the state. It is questionably unlikely that they would be so open to some of these concepts if the incidents that preceded the research had been different. If they had not understood that they narrowly escaped being fired by the state subsequent to the firing of the entire administrative staff, the research on this campus might have never been allowed (Steffe, 1990). This researcher understands that this research is far from a panacea, did not miss the opportunity to encourage the instructors to never miss any opportunity that might help one stay informed or curious enough to inquire themselves into new methods of doing things (Hoch & Dreyfus, 2007). This researcher was told that the rapport established by working very hard to be tactful, especially when discussing the other subjects, the students, which was needed on all sides, and always being willing to quickly contribute any data that relieved teachers' feelings of self-reproach finally produced the candidness that this type of research mandated. This researcher concludes that it actually allowed the mixed qualitative/ quantitative quality that was needed for more accuracy and more relevance.

With all of these changes, both the faculty and the students were sort of adrift. The research would have also been "adrift" had it not been nailed down to some firm scientific concepts and procedures (Fisher 1918). It was the old-fashioned students' t test that proved most true (Neyman and Pearson Part I, 1928; Neyman and Pearson Part II, 1928). It is to be concluded that H_0 can be rejected and that a p value of 0.02 is far less than our alpha of 0.05 (Personal communication D r. Eric Seuss). It is better to focus on this. We may be making headway in our Title One Tier Two School of Union High School to say that Algebra II is doing better at Structure Sense than Geometry and that we hope that we have shown that we can quantify this (Neyman and Pearson 1928).

Implications for Practice and Future Research

It is also just as true that neither class did as well as we would have hoped, but we all have made a showing. The real implication for practice and for future research is that these results, to be of any use, must influence the Mathematics Framework, Standards, and Curriculum. They must filter down to a professional development topic. The implementation might have to both be bottom up and top down. The definitions of the reasoning skills and other pertinent vocabulary need to be provided to the practicing professional. Leads in the form of a working annotated bibliography should be made available at these gatherings, even if it does no more then stir the curiosity. An incentive to actively read this annotated bibliography brings one's full understanding of these concepts to a math department staff meeting would also prove invaluable.

California is a state that is ripe for change and open to suggestion. Any future research will hopefully be able to tie these concepts into already existing assessments for both subjects, such as the Star Test for the students and the currently administered CSET examinations for the instructors. This is one of the many ideal top down approaches. The sample sizes used, twenty-one and twenty-seven, the grade levels used in this research, tenth to twelfth grade, were very demonstrative of an actual classroom setting. This research, like most others, could benefit from repeated trials in different districts but not a change in the actual parameters used here. The teachers' contribution as a subject is only as accurate as the follow-up interview. Future trials should keep these recommendations in mind.

References

Barak, M. & Shakman, L. (2007). Quality instruction creates high student learning. U rasian Journal of Mathematics, Science, and Technology Education, 4(1), 11-20.

Bodovski, K. & Farkas, G. (2007). Do instructional practices contribute to inequality in achievement? Journal of Early Childhood Research, 5, 301-322.

Boero, P. (2001). Transformation and anticipation as key processes in problem solving. In Perspectives on School Algebra (pp 99-119). Dorderecht, The Netherlands. Kluwer Academic Publishers.

Cifarelli, V.V. (1988). The role of abstraction as a learning process in mathematical problem solving. (Unpublished doctoral dissertation). Purdue University, Indiana.

Cooney, T. J. (1999). Conceptualizing teachers' way of knowing. Educational Studies in Mathematics, 38(1/ 3), 163-187.

Creswell, J. W. (2009). Qualitative inquiry and research design: Choosing among five approaches (3rd ed.). Thousand Oaks, C A: Sage.

Carling-Hammond, L . (2003). Enhancing teaching. In W. A. O wings, & L .

S. Kaplan (Eds.), Best practices, best thinking, and emerging issues in school leadership (pp. 75-87). Thousand Oaks, CA: Corwin Press.

D ole, S. (2003). Applying psychological theory to helping students overcome learned difficulties in mathematics. An alternative approach to intervention.

School Psychology International. 24(1), 95-114.

Driscoll, M. P. (2004). Psychology of learning for instruction (3rd ed.). Boston: Pearson.

Dreyfus T. & Eisenberg T. (1996) O different faucets of mathematical thinking. In The Nature of Mathematical Thinking. (pp.253-284). Mahwah, NJ, USA: Lawrence Ehrlbaum and Associates.

Faulkner, V. N. (2009, May/June). The components of number sense: An instructional model. Teaching Exceptional Children, 41(5), 24-31.

Ferrari, P. L. (2003, July 29). Abstractions in mathematics. Philosophical Transactions: Biological Sciences, The Abstraction Paths: From Experience to Concept, 358(1435), 1225-1230.

Fisher, R. A. (1918). The Correlation Between Relatives on the Supposition of Mendelian Inheritance. Philosophical Transactions of the Royal Society of Edinburgh, 52, 399-433.

Flores, S. & Flores, W. (2008, December). Productive strategies for raising student achievement in algebra: A personal view from two high school principals. NASSP Bulletin, 92, 305-315.

Fuhrman, S. H. & Odden, A. (2001). Introduction to a Kappan special section on school reform. Phi Delta Kappan, 83(1), 59-61.

Gonzales, P., Williams, T., Jocelyn, L., Roey, S., Kastberg, D., & Brenwald, S. (2008). Highlights from TIMSS 2007: Mathematics and science achievement of U.S. fourth-and eighth-grade students in an international context (NCES 2009-001). Washington, DC: National Center for Education Statistics, Institute of Education Sciences, U.S. Department of Education.

Gonzalves, P. (2008, July). Summer institute for math teachers. California State University at East Bay.

Goodson-Espy, T. (1998). The role of reification and reflective abstraction in the development of abstract thought: Transition from arithmetic to algebra. Educational Studies in Mathematics, 36, 219-245.

Gregory, G. & Chapman, C. (2007). Differentiated instructional strategies:

One size doesn't fit all (2nd ed.). Thousand Oaks, CA: Corwin Press.

Hazzan, O. & Zazkis, R. (2005). Reducing abstraction: The case of school mathematics. Educational Studies in Mathematics, 58(1), 101-119.

Henningson, M. & Stein, M. K. (1997). Mathematical tasks and student cognition. Journal for Research in Mathematical Education, 28, 524-549.

Hoch, M. (2003). Structure sense. In Proceedings for the Third C onference for European R esearch in Mathematics Education. Belleria, Italy : C E RME.

H och, M. & D reyfus, T. (2004). Structure sense in high school algebra: T he effect of brackets. In Proceedings of the 28th Conference of the International Group for the Psychology of Mathematics Education (vol 3 pp. 49-56) Bergen: N orway.

H och, M. & D reyfus, T. (2005). Students' difficulties with applying a familiar formula in an unfamiliar context. Proceedings of the 29th C onference of the I nternational Group for the Psychology of Mathematics Education, 3, 145-152.

Hoch, M. & Dreyfus, T. (2006). Structure sense versus manipulation skills: An unexpected result. Proceedings 30th C onference of the I nternational Group for the Psychology of Mathematics E ducation, 3, 305-312.

H och, M. & D reyfus, T. (2007). Recognizing an algebraic structure. Tel Aviv U niversity of I srael Cerme, 5, 436-446.

Izsak, A. (2000). Inscribing the winch: Mechanisms by which students develop knowledge structures for representing the physical world with algebra. The Journal of Learning Sciences, 9(1), 31-74.

Kamens, D. H., Meyer, J. W., & Benavot, A. (1996, May). Worldwide patterns in academic secondary education curricula. C omparative Education R eview, 40(2), 116-138.

L alley, J. P. & Miller, R. H . (n.d.). E ffects of Pre-Teaching and Re-Teaching on Math Achievement and Academic Self-Concept of Students with Low

Achievement in Math. In Journal of I nstructional Psychology. (Reprinted from

Journal E ducational Psychology, 2006, 4, [126], pp. 747-755.)

Leedy, P. D. & Ormrod, J. E. (2005). *Practical research: Planning and design* (8th ed.). Saddle River, NJ: Merrill Prentice Hall.

Linchevski, L. & Livneh, D. (1999). Structure sense: The relationship between algebra and numerical context. *Educational Studies in Mathematics, 40*(2), 173-196.

Lovat, T. & Toomey, R. (2009). *Values education and quality teaching: The double helix effect.* Dardest, The Netherlands: Springer Verlag.

Marzano, R. J. (2003). Curriculum and Instruction: Critical and Emerging Issues for Educational Leadership. In W. A. Owings, & L. S. Kaplan (Eds.), *Best practice, best thinking and emerging issues in school leadership* (pp. 65-73). Thousand Oaks, CA: Corwin Press.

Mayrowetz, D. (2009, July). Instructional practice in the context of converging policies: Teaching mathematics in inclusive elementary classrooms in the standards reform era. *Educational Policy, 23,* 554-588.

McCombs, B. L., Daniels, D. H., & Perry, K. E. (2008). Children's and teachers' perceptions of learner-centered practices and student motivation: Implications for early schooling. *The Elementary School Journal, 109*(1), 16-35.

Minitab. (2011). Retrieved from http://www.minitab.com/en-US/default.aspx

Moustakes, C. (1994). *Phenomenological research methods.* Thousand Oaks, CA: Sage Publications.

Nathan, M. J. & Koedinger, K. R. (2000a). An investigation of teachers' beliefs of students' algebra development. *Cognition and Instruction, 18,* 209237.

National Center for Education Statistics (2007). *Trends in International Mathematics and Science Study (TIMSS).* Retrieved May 29, 2009, from http://nces.ed.gov/timss/results07_math07.asp

Neyman, J. & Pearson, E. S. (1928, July). On the Use and Interpretation of Certain Test Criteria for Purposes of Statistical Inference Part I. *Biometrika, 20A* (½), 75-240, 207, 232.

Neyman, J. & Pearson, E. S. (1928, December/January). On the Use and Interpretation of Certain Test Criteria for Purposes of Statistical Inference Part II. Biometrika, 20A (3/4), 263-295.

N euman, W. L . (2007). Social research methods: Qualitative and quantitative approaches (5th ed.). Boston, MA: Pearson E ducation.

NCTM (National Council of Teachers of Mathematics). (2004). Overview: Standards for Grades 9-12. Retrieved N ovember 15, 2009, from http://standards.nctm.org/ document/ chapter7/ index.htm.

Novotna, J. & H och, M. (2008). H ow structure sense of algebraic expressions or equations is related to structure sense for abstract algebra. Mathematics Education R esearch Journal, 20(2), 93-104.

N umber Sense. (2007). Mathematics C ontent Standards for C alifornia Public Schools (p 8, 10, 13, 20, 24, 29, 33, 38) Retrieved from http:/ / www.cde.ca.

gov/ be/ st/ ss/ documents/ mathstandard.pdf

Patton, M. Q. (2002). Qualitative research and evaluation methods(3rd ed.). T housand O aks: Sage Publications.

Pierce, R. & Stacey, K . (2001) A framework for algebraic insight. I n N umeracy and Beyond. Proceedings of the 24th A nnual C onference of the Mathematics Education R esearch Group of A ustralia. (vol. 2 pp.418-425) Sydney Australia:

ME RGA.

Polly, D . (2008). Modeling the influence of calculator use and teacher effects on first grade students' mathematics achievement. Journal of Computers in Mathematics and Science Teaching, 27, 245-263.

Quinn, (1997). Effects of mathematics methods courses on the mathematical attitudes and content knowledge of preservice teachers. Journal of Educational R esearch. Retrieved from http://search.ebscohost.com/ login.aspx?direct=true&db=qeh&AN=BEDI98023102&site=ehost-live.

Reys, R. E. (2003, January). Assessing the impact of standards based middle grades mathematics curriculum materials on student achievement. Journal for R esearch in Mathematics Education, 34(1), 74-95.

Reys, R. E. (1984, May). *Mental computation and estimation: Past, present and future.* The Elementary School Journal, 84(5), 546-557.

Rubin, H .J. & Rubin, I.S. (2005). *Qualitative interviewing: The art of hearing data* (2nd ed.). T housand O aks, C A: Sage Publications.

Salkind, N.J. (2003). *Exploring research.* Upper Saddle River, NJ: Prentice H all.

Sebrecht, M. M., Enright, M., Bennett, R. E., & Martin, K. (1996). *Using algebra word problems to assess quantitative ability: Attributes, strategies, and errors.* C ognition and I nstruction, 14(3), 285-343.

Sfard, A. (1994, March). *The gains and pitfalls of reification: The case of algebra.* Educational Studies in Mathematics, 26(2/ 3), 191-228.

Sfard, A. & Linchevski, L. (1994). *The gains and pitfalls of reification. The case for algebra.* Educational Studies in Mathematics, 26, 191-228.

Steffe, L . P. (1990). *O n the knowledge of mathematics teachers.* Journal for Research in Mathematics Education, 4, 167-210. Retrieved from http:/ / www.csueastbay.edu

D r. E ric Seuss, C hair of Statistics C alifornia State U niversity of the E ast Bay, Hayward, California Campus. 25800 Carlos Bee Blvd, - 94542 Personal C ommunication, D ecember 2, 2010. Phone 510-885-3000.

SurveyMonkey. (2010) *Help Center- Analyze section.* Retrieved from http:/ / help.surveymonkey.com/ app/ answers/ detail/ a_id/ 270/ ~/ the-analyze-section-shows-statistical-data-in-the-form-of-summary-numbers%2Ftext.

Taylor, S. J. & Bogdan, R. (1998). *Introduction to qualitative methods* (3rd ed.). N ew York, N Y: John Wiley.

T hompson, A.G. (2004). *T he relationship of teachers' conceptions of mathematics and mathematics teaching to instructional practices.* In Allen, B. & Johnston-Wilder, S. (Eds.), Mathematics education: Exploring the culture of learning (pp. 175-186). Routledge Falmer, N ew York: N Y.

T horpe, M. (2003). *C ollaborative on-line learning: Transforming learner support and course design.* In Tait, a., & Mills, R. (Eds.).

Re-thinking learner support in distance education, pp. 219-228. London, UK: Routledge Falmer.

Triol, M. (2006). Elementary statistics (10th ed.). Boston: Addison Wesley.

U.S. Department of Education. (2001). No Child Left Behind Act, Pub. L.

No 107-110, 115 STAT. 1425 (2002).

U.S. Department of Education (2008). The Nation's Report Card: National assessment of educational progress. Retrieved July 5, 2009, from http://nces.ed.gov/nationareportcard/faq.asp#ques1

U.S. Department of Health and Human Services Code of Federal Regulations, 45 CFR § 46.102(2009).

Van Dooren, W. V., Verschaffel, L., & Onghena, P. (2002, November). The impact of preservice teachers' content knowledge on their evaluation of students' strategies for solving arithmetic and algebra word problems. Journal for Research in Mathematics Education, 33(5), 319-351.

White-Clark, R., DiCarlo, M., & Gilchriest, S. N. (2008, April/May). Guide on the side: An instructional approach to meet mathematics standards. The High School Journal, 6, 40-44.

White, P. A., Gamoran, A., Smithson, J., & Porter, A. C. (1996). Upgrading the high school math course-taking patterns in seven high schools in California and New York. Educational Evaluation and Policy Analysis, 18(4), 285307.

Student's t-test (2011) Retrieved from http://en.wikipedia.org/wiki/Student%27s_t-test#Unpaired_and_paired_two-sample_t-tests and distribution tables also obtained from Wikipedia on the Internet.

Wilkins, J. L. (2008). The relationship among elementary teachers' content knowledge, attitudes, beliefs, and practices. Journal of Mathematics Teacher Education, 11(1), 139-164.

Woodward, J. (2004, January/February). Mathematics education in the United States: Past to present. Journal of Learning Disabilities, 37(16), 16-31.

Yin, R. K. (2003). Case study research (2nd ed.). Thousand Oaks, CA: Sage.

Zimmerman, B. J., & Dibenedetto, M. K. (2008). Mastery learning and assessment: Implications for students and teachers in an era of high-stakes testing. Psychology in the Schools, 45, 206-217.

Appendices

— Appendix A: Letter of Consent to Conduct Study

— Appendix B: Instructor Survey

— Appendix C : Student Constructed Response Worksheets

— I

— II

— III

Appendix A:
Letter of Consent to Conduct Study

INFORMED CONSENT TO PARTICIPATE IN A RESEARCH STUDY
(Impact of Reasoning Skills on Algebra V Geometry)

A. PURPOSE AND BACKGROUND

The purpose of this research study is to ascertain the effects of reasoning skills on Algebra V students and the subsequent effect on Geometry.

The researcher, Lisa Johnson, is a graduate student at East Bay (conducting research for a Master's degree/honor's thesis.)

You are being asked to participate in this study because you teach Algebra II or Geometry.

B. PROCEDURES

If you agree to participate in this research study, the following will occur:

- You will take an 18 question multiple choice survey that will be delivered to your email address.

- You will be interviewed for approximately 5 minutes about your follow-up concerns.

- Field notes will be taken to ensure accuracy in reporting your statements.

- The interview will take place at a time convenient for you.

- The researcher may contact you later to clarify your interview answers.

- Total time commitment will be 25 minutes.

C. RISKS

There is a risk of loss of privacy. However, no names or identities will be used in any published reports of the research. Only the researcher will have access to the research data.

D. CONFIDENTIALITY

The research data will be kept in a secure location (or/password protected program), and only the researcher will have access to the data. At the conclusion of the study, all identifying information will be removed and the data will be kept in a locked cabinet or office and destroyed after 3 years. Audiotapes will be destroyed at the end of the study.

E. DIRECT BENEFITS

There will be no direct benefits to the participant.

F. COSTS

There will be no cost to you for participating in this research.

G. COMPENSATION

There will be no compensation for participating in this research.

H. QUESTIONS

If you have any questions about the study, you may contact the researcher by email at ljohnson58@horizon.csueastbay.edu, or phone at (510) 3290017. Questions about your rights as a study participant, or comments or complaints about the study, may be addressed to the Office of Research and Sponsored Programs at (510) 885-4212.

I. CONSENT

You have been given a copy of this consent form to keep.

PARTICIPATION IN THIS RESEARCH IS VOLUNTARY. You are free to

decline to participate in this research study, or to withdraw your participation at any point, without penalty. Your decision whether or not to participate in this research study will have no influence on your present or future status.

Signature _____ *Date:*_____

Researcher Parcticipant

Signature _____ *Date:*_____

Researcher Parcticipant

Appendix B: Instructor Survey

Math Reasoning Skills Exit this survey

1. Copy of page: Default Section
1. Is secondary mathematics your area of content knowledge?
   o   Yes-Explain _____

   _____

   _____

   o   No-Explain _____

   _____

   _____

   o   Other-Explain _____

   _____

   _____

2. How long have you taught Secondary Mathematics?
   o   1-3 Years-Explain_____

   _____

   _____

   o   4-10 Years-Explain_____

   _____

   _____

   o   Greater Than 10 Years-Explain_____

   _____

   _____

3. How comfortable are you teaching Mathematics?
   o   Very Comfortable-Explain_____
   _____
   _____

   o   Somewhat Comfortable-Explain_____
   _____
   _____

   o   Not Comfortable at all-Explain_____
   _____
   _____

4. Can you define Number Sense?
   o   Yes-Explain _____
   _____
   _____

   o   No-Explain _____
   _____
   _____

   o   With help (i.e Textbook)-Explain _____
   _____
   _____

5. Can you define structure sense?
    o   Yes-Explain _____
    _____
    _____

    o   No-Explain _____
    _____
    _____

6. Can you define abstract reasoning?
    o   Yes-Explain _____
    _____
    _____

    o   No-Explain _____
    _____
    _____

    o   With help (i.e Textbook)-Explain _____
    _____
    _____

7. Can number sense be taught in a standard Mathematics class?
    o   Yes-Explain _____
    _____
    _____

    o   No-Explain _____
    _____
    _____

    o   With help (i.e Textbook)-Explain _____
    _____

8. Can structure sense be taught in a standard classroom setting?
    o   Yes-Explain _____

    _____

    o   No-Explain _____

    _____

    o   With help (i.e Textbook)-Explain _____

    _____

9. C an abstract reasoning be taught in a standard classroom?
    o   Yes-Explain _____

    _____

    o   No-Explain _____

    _____

    o   With help (i.e Textbook)-Explain _____

    _____

10. Can some aspect of learned number sense be evaluated in a standard classroom by the instructor?
    - Yes-Explain _____
    _____
    _____
    - No-Explain _____
    _____
    _____
    - With help (i.e Textbook)-Explain _____
    _____
    _____

11. Can some aspect of learned structure sense be evaluated in a standard classroom by the instructor?
    - Yes-Explain _____
    _____
    _____
    - No-Explain _____
    _____
    _____
    - With help (i.e Textbook)-Explain _____
    _____
    _____

12. Can some aspect of learned abstract reasoning be evaluated in a standard classroom by the instructor?
- o   Yes-Explain _____
  _____
  _____
- o   No-Explain _____
  _____
  _____
- o   With help (i.e Textbook)-Explain _____
  _____
  _____

13. Where did you learn about number sense? Check all that apply.
- o   High School/College-explain_____
  _____
  _____
- o   Preservice/Methods -Explain_____
  _____
  _____
- o   Professional Development-Explain _____
  _____
  _____

14. Where did you learn about Structure Sense? Check all that apply.
   o   High School/College-explain_____
   _____
   _____

   o   Preservice/Methods -Explain_____
   _____
   _____

   o   Professional Development-Explain _____
   _____
   _____

15. Where did you learn about Abstract Reasoning? Check all that apply.
   o   High School/College-explain_____
   _____
   _____

   o   Preservice/Methods -Explain_____
   _____
   _____

   o   Professional Development-Explain _____
   _____
   _____

Appendix C:
Student Constructed Response Worksheets

Name/ Identifyer:_____
Date: _____
Student Constructed Response: Structure Sense I

Show All Work
Factor: $81-(x^2)$

Name/ Identifyer:_____

Date: _____

Student Constructed Response: Structure Sense II

Show All Work

Factor: $64x^4y^4$

Solve: $5(3x-14)^2 = 20$

Factor: $6(5-x) + 2x(5-x)$

The Impact on Algebra vs. Geometry of a Learner's Ability to Develop

Reasoning Skills

Name/Identifyer _____

Date _____

Student Constructed Response: Structure Sense III

Show All Work

Simplify: (x^3+x)

(x^2+1)

Solve: $x^2 + 4x + 4 = 0$

www.ingramcontent.com/pod-product-compliance
Lightning Source LLC
Chambersburg PA
CBHW030916080526
44589CB00010B/335